# LOW RISK METHOD TO MAKE MILLIONS IN WALL STREET

BY: AN INVESTMENT ADVISOR / M.D.

Registration Number : TXu 2-180-469

Title of Work:  LOW RISK METHOD TO MAKE MILLIONS IN WALL STREET

Year of Completion: 2020

Author: An Investment Advisor/M.D.

Effective Date of Registration: January 14, 2020

# DISCLAIMER

This book is intended for educational purposes only. Investing in securities like stocks, mutual funds, options, futures, commodities and others carry significant risk. If you need professional investment advice you should consult a registered investment advisor and a financial planner. This book contains the author's opinions. The author does not have any financial interest in any of the business entities or companies mentioned in this book. The author may own some of the securities mentioned in this book. This book is sold with the understanding that neither the author nor the publisher is engaged in rendering financial, legal, accounting or other professional services. If you need any of these services, you should seek the advice of a professional person. You should consider virtual/paper trading before investing your hard-earned money. You should consider the possible risks of investing in the stock market and consider your investment goals and risk tolerance before investing. You should understand that past performance does not guarantee future results. By reading this book you are implicitly agreeing to these terms. Past performance of the stock market is not a guarantee for future results.

# DEDICATION

This book is dedicated to all the wizards of Wall Street from whom I have learnt an unbelievable amount of knowledge!

# CONTENTS

# WHAT WILL YOU FIND IN THIS BOOK?

Potentially this book can make millions for you. In 2014 approximately $14 trillion were invested in the U.S. stock market. In 2018 it has grown to $33 trillion. Thus, more money is chasing approximately the same number of stocks. For you to make money in the market, you need a technique or method. If you do not have a method you will be thrown into the arena with lions. Listen, you are competing with professionals who are investing millions of dollars and using ultra-fast super computers. Investments from individuals constitute only 15%. This book gives you a clear and concise method which will make you succeed and make millions without losing sleep. This method is based on long term investing and you should give at least fifteen years to achieve the goal. This is based on the beauty of compounding of growth which is the road to riches. The wealthy know what compounding does.

## ABOUT THE AUTHOR

The author is a retired mutual fund manager and an associate clinical professor of medicine.

## ONE REQUEST

If you find this book to be useful, kindly recommend to others via social networking media. This gesture is greatly appreciated. Also please show this book to your accountant for a second opinion. I showed it to my accountant for his opinion, confirmation and comments. He liked it and started applying this strategy in his accounts.

# GOAL

Create profits

Grow your assets

Retire rich

Enjoy the fruits of profits

Help the needy

# GOLDEN WORDS OF WISDOM

Do not believe in anything simply because you have heard it. Do not believe in anything simply because it is spoken and rumored by many. Do not believe in anything simply because it is found written in books. Do not believe in anything merely on the authority of your elders. Do not believe in traditions because they have been handed down for many generations. But after OBSERVATION and ANALYSIS, when you find that anything AGREES WITH REASON, then accept it and live up to it.

(Would you believe that these words were uttered around 2500 years ago by Gautama Buddha and they apply so well to the stock market today?)

# SEVEN PEARLS FOR SUCCESS

Success in investing is similar to stringing a pearl necklace. Any missing pearl can break the necklace.

You need the following 7 pearls:

1. Understanding yourself
2. Understanding the market
3. Right information
4. Right tools
5. Common sense
6. Sticking to rules rigidly
7. Nerves of steel

# FOREWORD

Hello fellow investors: This book is especially created to help you retire as millionaires.

You have spent many years learning. You may have huge student loans to pay.

You work very hard and long hours. You cannot allot six to eight hours a week for investments.

You are trusting. So, there are people who take you for a ride.

You do not have time to waste with regards to investing. You have to start investing as early as possible; sooner the better as your money will have more time to grow. Time is of essence so that you will have a bundle of money when you retire. You can relax and enjoy after years of hard work. You need the right investment to retire rich. No one else cares as much as you do with regards to your money! You take charge and be the pilot.

It is never too late to start. If you have at least 5 years before retirement, you can follow this method. You need 5 years because there could be a bear market soon after you start investing. But bear markets do not last forever. They end in bull markets.

There is lot of money that can be made in Wall Street. For example, Warren Buffett started a limited partnership in 1957. He raised $105,000 in capital and he was the general partner. As of 9/17/2019 his Berkshire Hathaway A shares had a market capitalization of nearly $516 billion! Wow!! The main reasons for his success are 1. Buying stocks or companies at fair or bargain prices. 2. Holding on to them for many years so that earnings and the yields are compounded. What Warren Buffett looks for is an investment that will give him the largest annual return on his capital. Year over year when the returns are compounded the results become astonishing. "Warren believes that compounding is the secret to getting really rich". (Buffettolgy by Mary Buffett & David Clark)

The following is another quotation from the same book. "If your investments grow at 15% to 25% a year, if you started with $1 million, in 30 years, you will have, max, $807 million... What? No...... 807 billion dollars!!!"

As of January of 2018 the market capitalization of the US stock market was around $33 trillion. In 2014 it was only $ 18 trillion. More money is chasing the same number of stocks. The richest people in the world invest in the U.S. stock market with only one goal, to make money.

Yes. You can make lot of money consistently if you follow a method. If you do not have a method, you will be thrown into the arena with lions. Listen, you are competing with professionals who are investing millions of dollars, using fast computers, thus controlling the market. If you do not have a formula, you can become a millionaire very quickly, if you started as a billionaire!!

I am going to give you a method/formula which will make you huge amounts of money if you are disciplined. This method is based on the BEAUTY OF COMPOUNDING. It is an extremely powerful tool.

The rich Medici family in Italy Invested funds equal to $100,000, six hundred years ago. The funds grew at 5% annually.

It grew to five hundred and seventeen quadrillions ($517,100,000,000,000,000). Reported by Frank A. Vanderlip in 1933. Amazing!!

What you need is time on your side for your investment to grow. The investment should be good, stable and powerful and has proven by making good profits year over year (compounded growth). In this book you will find your answer and the secret to success. You do not need any other outside help. You trust in yourself and in this book and follow the guidelines to success.

Lot of people lose money by trading in the stock market because they do not have a method. There is too much information out there. You need the right information to make money.

## SUMMARY

- You can make millions in Wall Street if you rigidly follow a method.
- Compounding is the secret to getting filthy rich.
- You need at least fifteen years to achieve a huge amount for your retirement.
- You should use a tax deferred account in a solid brokerage company.

# FOREWORD BY TWO CPAs

Every investor should read "LOW RISK METHOD TO MAKE MILLIONS IN WALL STREET" before investing another dollar in the stock market. It's a much needed remedy for all the foolish mistakes, short-sighted moves, and investment ills that routinely plague most individual investors left to follow their own whims--or worse, the advice of their investment brokers and financial advisors, who seem to have an uncanny knack for losing clients' money even in a roaring bull market! In the many years that I have been an accountant and tax practitioner, I have seen firsthand the results: Rarely do individual investors consistently make money over the long term. The stock market, it seems, is not like any other consumer market. Here individual shoppers sell in a panic when prices are low, and rush in to buy when prices are high--a certain prescription for financial disaster! This book provides an antidote to this nonsense by offering a sound, but simple, solution to the problem of how to invest wisely for the long term. So, turn off the computer, hang up the phone, shut the TV, and read "LOW RISK METHOD TO MAKE MILLIONS IN WALL STREET". It might be the best investment move you have ever made.

**Raymond Tse & Stephen Apolito,**
CPAs VB&T Certified Public Accountants,
PLLC 250 W 57th St Suite 1632 New York,
NY 10107 T.212-448-0010
F.888-99-PCAOB (72262)
http://getcpa.com

# FOREWORD BY A 3rd CPA

This is an excellent book for professionals who are busy in their professions and don't have the time to watch the stock market on a regular basis. I wish I had applied the advice suggested in this book 20 years ago rather than timing the market. But as the author's work demonstrates, it is never too late to get started. I also strongly encourage readers to invest in their retirement accounts to maximize the returns and make a commitment to investing regularly whether it is weekly, monthly, quarterly or annually. The use of retirement accounts is most tax-efficient because by delaying the payment of income taxes you are compounding the returns on a larger portion of the investment.

Best wishes,

**Roger Idnani, CPA, MST, MBA**
Professor Department of Accounting,
Mihaylo College of Business & Economics,
California State University Fullerton,
Tel: 1-714-791-2691
Email: Ridnani@fullerton.edu

## INTRODUCTION

This book will focus on a specific ETF (Exchange Traded Fund) and a specific method to achieve the goal of making millions of dollars for your retirement. It is designed for you hard working people who do not have free time in your hands.

Let me ask you something. How many methods do you need to make millions?............ Only one!!

This book is like a diamond, small yet invaluable!

# BROKERAGE

First of all, let us select a brokerage which is one of the top-rated ones; one that is financially in good shape; one that offers no fee ETFs for online trades I came up with three names: Charles Schwab, TDAmeritrade and E*Trade. These are all highly rated reputable companies. They all offer free online trades for ETFs. As you pay no commissions for your trades, all the money you invest goes into your account. Every drop counts in the long run.

As per Yahoo Finance on 10/7/2019, Charles Schwab has a debt/equity of 45%. E*Trade Financial has debt/equity of 44%. TDAmeritrade has debt/equity of 42%. This list is growing. If you Google you will find more brokerage firms that offer free online trading of ETFs. When you open an account with any other company check on their debt/equity ratio to see how strong the company is.

Your accounts are insured by SIPC (Securities Investor Protection Corporation). What does SIPC protect? Please make sure that your brokerage account is protected by SIPC. Some brokerage firms offer additional insurance on their own. You have to find out the insurance coverage on your accounts. This is important, because if your brokerage firm becomes troubled financially, your account will be protected up to $500,000 which includes $250,000 in cash. Your account is not protected for fluctuations in the market value of your securities. Money market mutual funds are considered as securities and not as cash. So, once your account value goes above $500,000, you should open a second account in another brokerage firm.

SIPC coverage of $500,000 is extended to each "legal customer." For instance, if you have three accounts at a firm-and one is an individually held account in your name only, another is a joint account with your spouse, and a third is an IRA account in your name-each account is considered a separate "legal customer" and each will be eligible for full SIPC coverage.

Brokerage firms are required to follow certain rules that are designed to minimize the chances of financial failure and, more importantly, to protect customer assets if they do fail. For example, the SEC's Rule 15c3-1-the "Net Capital Rule"-requires brokerage firms to maintain certain levels of their own liquid assets. The minimum net capital a firm must have on hand depends on its size and business.

In addition, the SEC's Rule 15c3-3-the "Customer Protection Rule"-requires brokerage firms that have custody of customer assets to keep those assets separate from their own accounts. In other words, customers' cash must be placed in a special, separate "reserve" account; and fully paid customer securities must be kept separate from firm and customer margin securities. Please read the following:
https://www.finra.org/investors/alerts/if-brokerage-firm-closes-its-doors

## SUMMARY

- This book will focus on a specific ETFs and a specific method to achieve our goal.
- You need to open a retirement account in a reputable, financially strong brokerage company which offers free online ETF trading.
- You have to check about the insurance on your account. You may have to open more than one account in different firms so that your retirement accounts are protected by SIPC.

# WHAT IS AN EXCHANGE TRADED FUND OR ETF?

It is a collection of securities. The ETF tracks the underlying index of securities. The credit goes to Canada for starting the world's first ETF in 1990 for creating a pooled investment vehicle which can be traded like a stock. This has caused a revolution. The first ETF in the USA was started in 1993. Investing in individual stocks is risky and so the demand for ETFs has been growing all the time. Both individual and institution investors invest increasingly into ETFs. As of March of 2019 there are more than 5000 ETFs. Wow! This number has been growing steadily.

Blackrock, Inc. is the largest company managing over 800 ETFs with a market capitalization of over $ 1 trillion. The Vanguard group is the second largest with regards to ETFs and has a market capitalization of also over $1 trillion. There many other smaller firms which manage ETFs.

There are different types of ETFs and I will you some examples. There are regular ETFs like QQQ. QQQ invests in NASDAQ-100, which consists of 100 largest capitalized stocks in NASDAQ. When NASDAQ-100 goes up by 1%, QQQ will go up by 1%.

There are contra ETFs. One example is PSQ. When NASDAQ-100 goes up by 1%, PSQ will go down by 1%. There are 2X leveraged regular ETFs. An example is QLD. When NASDAQ-100 goes up by 1%, QLD will go up by 2%. An example of 2X leveraged contra ETF is QID. When NASDAQ-100 goes up by $1, QID will go down by $2.

There are 3X leveraged regular ETFs like TQQQ. When NASDAQ-100 goes up by 1%, TQQQ will go up by 3%. An example of 3X leveraged contra ETF is SQQQ. When NASDAQ-100 goes up by 1%, SQQQ will go down by 3%. Thus, there are numerous regular, 2X leveraged and 3X leveraged ETFs in the market.

There are several categories of ETFs: 1. Index ETFs (for example small cap, mid cap, large cap, multi cap. QQQ is a large cap ETF). 2. Stock ETFs (for e.g. a stock ETF will have stocks in its portfolio). 3. Sector ETFs (for e.g. energy sector ETF, biotechnology ETF, etc.). 4. Foreign ETFs. 5. Bond ETFs. 6. Currency ETFs.

## SUMMARY

- As of March 2019 there are over 5000 ETFs and their number is growing.
- There are regular ETFs, contra ETFs, leverage ETFs  small cap ETFs, midcap ETFs, large cap ETFs, stock ETFs, sector ETFs, bond ETFs, currency ETFs, foreign ETFs, global ETFs, etc.

# WHY SHOULD YOU INVEST IN ETFs?

The costs of holding ETFs are quite low. For e.g. the annual expense ratio of QQQ is 0.20%. There is a dividend yield of around 0.78%. So, it is net positive. You can buy or sell ETF intraday. On a $100,000 investment the annual expense ratio of QQQ is 0.20% as of September 2019 and it amounts to $200. On the positive side $100,000 investment will collect a dividend yield of 0.78% which adds up to $780. You come out ahead with a net gain of 0.58% or $580. No bad! The approximate annual cost of owning a mutual fund is around $1250 for an investment of $100,000.

In case you own a mutual fund you cannot liquidate your assets intraday. You can get only end of the day net asset value pricing. When you own QQQ there is usually less than 1% yield which is distributed annually. You will get a 1099 form which you have to file with your income tax returns. ETFs are more tax efficient than mutual funds. Most mutual funds do not beat S&P 500 index! Also the best mutual funds this year may not be on top in the next few years.

Also, stock ETFs own a number of stocks and so there is no individual stock risk. For example, QQQ tracks NASDAQ-100 and at this time there are 103 stocks in it. So, if one company goes bankrupt your portfolio will lose less than 1%. Owning individual stocks can be risky. For example, if you had lot of money invested in Enron, your whole investment would have been wiped out.

It is not good to gamble with your retirement money. Also, your money in an ETF like QQQ is invested in different industry groups and so if one industry group goes down it will not affect the entire investment. It gets buffered.

Also, the portfolio of any ETF is transparent. You can go to their website and find out the current portfolio. There are four major ETFs which are SPY, DIA, QQQ and IWM.

Now I will show you an ETF that has beaten SPY (which tracks S&P 500 index), DIA (ETF which tracks Dow Jones Industrial Average) and IWM (which tracks Russell 2000 small cap index) by a significant margin. It has five-star rating by Morningstar.

QQQ tracks NASDAQ-100 index. As of September of 2019, there are 103 stocks in NASDAQ-100 and if we add up all the market cap of these 103 stocks it is over $10 trillion. Amazing! When you invest in QQQ you are backed by stocks worth $10 trillion!

These stocks are invested in different industry groups. The old Wall Street adage is "Diversify, diversify, diversify". Yes. When you buy QQQ, your funds are diversified into different industry groups with a $ 10 trillion market cap!!  Wow! You can sleep peacefully at night.

"If you have a harem of a hundred girls, you never get to know any of them very well. The trick is to know a lot about what you own, and you don't own that many things". (Warren Buffett, one of the greatest investors of all times)

"The idea of focused investing has zero currency in academic circles. Investment managers don't feel they will make enough money this way. It is so foreign to them". (Charlie Munger)

## SUMMARY

- The cost of owning any ETF is very low compared to mutual funds.
- Unlike mutual funds, you can buy or sell an ETF intraday.
- When you own a stock ETF like QQQ you have no single stock risk. QQQ tracks NASDAQ-100 which has the largest capitalized stocks in NASDAQ.
- The market cap of NASDAQ-100 in September of 2019 is over $10 trillion.
- QQQ has beaten DIA, SPY and IWM by a significant margin from 2005 to 2019.

(Please see the table below)

| SYMBOL | START DATE | START PRICE | END DATE | END PRICE | % PRICE CHANGE | % ANNUALIZED RATE OF RETURN |
|--------|-----------|-------------|----------|-----------|----------------|------------------------------|
|        | 9/27/2004 |             | 9/27/2019 |          |                |                              |
| QQQ    |           | 34.5        |          | 187.03    | 442.12         | 29.46                        |
| BRKA   |           | 86.2        |          | 311.45    | 261.31         | 17.41                        |
| VTI    |           | 53.38       |          | 150.3     | 181.57         | 12.1                         |
| IWM    |           | 55.74       |          | 151.16    | 171.21         | 11.41                        |
| DIA    |           | 100.16      |          | 267.99    | 167.56         | 11.16                        |
| SPY    |           | 110.75      |          | 295.4     | 166.73         | 11.11                        |

QQQ is Invesco QQQ Trust

SPY is SPDR S&P 500 ETF

BRKA is Berkshire Hathaway A shares (in thousands)

VTI is Vanguard Total Stock Market Index ETF

IWM is iShares Russell 2000 Index ETF

DIA is SPDR Dow Jones Industrial Average ETF

# INVESCO QQQ TRUST

For data click this link (https://www.invesco.com/us-rest/contentdetail?contentId=3a48e01e98630410VgnVCM10000046f1bf0aRCRD&dnsName=us)

This book will focus on an ETF called QQQ only. That is all you need to make millions for your retirement. Among the major stock indices QQQ stands out in performance way above DIA, SPY, IWM, VTI, and BRKA.

QQQ is a regular ETF meaning that when NASDAQ 100 goes up by 1%, QQQ will go up by 1%. It is not leveraged and so the volatility is lower than that of leveraged index funds and you can hold it for decades. The ETFs listed below are related to QQQ which are leveraged and also contra. The other ETFs like DIA, SPY and IWM also have related leveraged and contra ETFs and we will not deal with any of them.

PSQ is a contra ETF and when NASDAQ 100 goes down by 1% PSQ goes up by 1%. QLD is 2X leveraged. When NASDAQ 100 goes up by 1% QLD will go up by 2%. QID is 2 x leveraged contra ETF and it goes up by 2% when NASDAQ 100 goes down by 1%. TQQQ is 3 x leveraged and TQQQ will go up by 3% if NASDAQ 100 goes up by 1%. SQQQ is 3 x leveraged and it goes up by 3% if NASDAQ 100 goes down by 1%.

The leveraged ETFs are meant only for trading on a short-term basis like 3 days and not for long term investing. These are compounded on a daily basis and their net asset accounting is closed every day. So, these ETFs will go up and down very fast.

Also, if you are invested in the wrong leveraged ETF you will lose significant amount of money in a hurry. For e.g. if you own a leveraged contra ETF like SQQQ and if QQQ goes up you will lose your investment in SQQQ very fast.

QQQ is managed by Invesco and is called QQQ Trust. Its inception date is 03/10/1999. Its expense ratio is 0.20%. This is very low when compared to mutual funds. There is also an annual yield of around 0.78%. Once in a while some stocks in NASDAQ 100 may be replaced by better ones. So, there are 100 large capitalized stocks and so there is no single stock risk when you own QQQ. You are investing in 100 stocks when you buy one share of QQQ. It is similar to buying 100 different stocks in your portfolio but you do not manage 100 different stocks which will be a formidable task.

When you invest in QQQ your life becomes simple, yet you are investing in 100 largest capitalized stocks in NASDAQ like Microsoft, Apple, Amazon, Facebook, Alphabet, Intel, Comcast, etc. The 30-day average trading volume of QQQ is around 27 million shares. So, you can buy or sell in a second. The spread between bid and ask is only a few cents. The ask is the price you pay when you buy. Bid is what you get when you sell. You are not going to sell QQQ until you retire at which time you will be a millionaire or billionaire and then start withdrawing from the nest egg.

The following information was obtained from Invesco website as of 9/17/2019. The following is the sector allocation of QQQ: Information Technology 45.42%, Communication Services 21.78%, Consumer Discretionary 16.20%, Health Care 7.47%, Consumer Staples 6.05%, Industrials 2.38%, Utilities 0.38%, Financial 0.30%.

QQQ is market capitalization weighted. This means that the companies with the largest market cap will have the highest weights in the index. (Market cap is calculated by multiplying the share price and the number of shares outstanding). The top holdings are: Microsoft Corp 11.11%, Apple Inc 10.76%, Amazon.com Inc 9.47%, Facebook Inc 4.80%, GOOG Alphabet Inc 4.6%, GOOGL Alphabet Inc 4.03%, Intel Corp 2.76%, Cisco Systems Inc 2.52%, Comcast Corp 2.47%, PepsiCo Inc 2.23%.

Return on Equity is an excellent 38.47%. Price/Earnings ratio is 22.68%. Its average market capitalization is $439,304 million. The total market capitalization of all the stocks listed in NASDAQ 100 index is around $10 trillion! QQQ tracks NASDAQ 100 index. QQQ is listed on the NASDAQ exchange. It uses options and short selling. Currently it holds 103 stocks. These are the largest capitalized stocks in all of NASDAQ. Always large cap stocks are much less risky when compared to all the other stocks.

QQQ has gone up in the past 15 years on an average of 29% per year which is extraordinary! As of September of 2019, its net assets are $74.3B. It's alpha in the past 3 years has been 4.02 which is great when compared to the category average of -0.19%.

What alpha means is that It has performed better than the comparable funds by 4.02%.

Its beta is 1.11 when compared to the market beta of 1. This means that the volatil ty as measured by beta is only slightly higher than the rest of the market. You can sleep over it.

"High quality equities have outperformed every other asset class over a twenty-year period". (Jeremy Siegel). QQQ represents one of the best among equities. QQQ has proven itself as an outstanding investment in the past 15 years. It is rated five star by Morn ngstar.

## SUMMARY

- QQQ tracks NASDAQ 100 which currently has different sectors.
- QQQ is market cap weighted and the market cap of the average stock is c ose to half a million dollars.
- QQQ has gone up by an average of 29% in the past 15 years which is superb.
- The volatility of QQQ is 1.1 when compared to the whole market volatility cf 1 which is not high. You can sleep over it.

# BEAUTY OF COMPOUNDING

It is the most powerful tool you will find in the investment world!

The rich Medici family in Italy invested funds equal to $100,000, six hundred years ago. The funds grew at 5% annually. It grew to five hundred and seventeen quadrillions. ($517,100,000,000,000,000). Wow! Reported by Frank A. Vanderlip in 1933. Amazing but true! Even though it grew only at 5% a year because of the snowballing effect over many years the result was mind boggling.

Your account will do the same thing if you are patient. When you retire you will have millions and the numbers will be Himalayan! The wealthy people know the effect of compounding. That is the way they get rich.

The method I am recommending is for the long term. It is based on compounding; the growth is added year over year. Please understand that you need a minimum of fifteen years to see a huge total number. The reason is that the stock market does not go up every day. It has its own mind and goes up and down all the time. You need time on your side for the compounding effect. In this method we do not care whether the market goes up or down. Every month or better every two weeks you keep buying the ETF called QQQ. Every time you buy QQQ the price would be different. Please do not pay attention to any news or the price of QQQ or where the market is. Your goal is to keep buying QQQ at fixed intervals and when you retire you would be super-duper rich. You have to have faith and strong will.

To be successful you cannot waver. You have to stick the plan firmly.

Try to invest in tax deferred plans like IRA, 401 K, Pension Trusts, etc. so that the growth is not taxed. Please listen to Warren Buffett. "If you like spending 6-8 hours per week working on investments, do it. If you don't then dollar-cost average into index funds. This accomplishes diversification across assets and time, two very important things".

**SUMMARY**

- Compounding is an extremely powerful tool and the rich know the beauty of it.
- Dollar-cost average into QQQ and after fifteen years you will hit a jackpot like number in your retirement account.

# STRATEGIES USING QQQ

Let us say that you start investing $ 6,000 a year starting at age 30 in IRA. You add $6,000 a year at the beginning of each year. (Or you can invest $500 a month and your final figure will be even bigger than investing once a year). Because of the ease of calculating I have used examples of investing once a year in the beginning of the year. The results will be different if you calculate using investment done once a year at the end of the year.

All you do is keep on buying only QQQ in your retirement account at the current price of QQQ. The growth rate in the past 15 years of QQQ has been 29%. I used the compound interest calculator found in www.moneychimp.com. Let us say, you start investing at age 30 and retire at 65; you invest $6000 a year in the beginning of the year in QQQ. Here are the findings: At 65 you will have $242,662,371! This is unbelievable but true. You can calculate it for yourself. You can ask your accountant to verify this. This is very similar to how cancer cells divide, double and grow to billions!

There are two main reasons for this phenomenal growth. One is due to the long period of 35 years, with growth on growth added every year. The other factor is the high growth rate of 29%. This growth rate is from 9/27/2004 to 9/27/2019 (fifteen years). This period includes the significant drop in the stock market in the 2008/2009 period.

The inception date of QQQ was 3/10/1999. I could calculate only from 4/23/1999 to 9/27/2019. On 4/23/1999 it was trading at $55.32. On 9/27/2019 it was trading at $187.03. During that period, it had gone up by 238.12% or at an annualized rate of 11.65%. This period includes the dotcom bust in year 2000. Even if you use the annualized growth rate of 11.65% and invest $6000 a year for 35 years you will still have $2,947,494. You will still be a millionaire. Of course, QQQ has been doing much better in the past 15 years in spite of the huge market correction in 2008-2009. This is because of the growth seen in companies like Microsoft, Apple, Amazon, Facebook, Google, etc. In year 2000 the drop in the market was due to irrational exuberance when people invested huge amounts of money in small worthless companies which led to the dotcom bubble and bust. If you study the list of companies in QQQ you will be impressed by the quality and strength of the underlying companies. These are not tiny companies. For example, Microsoft and Apple have market caps currently of over $1 trillion!

A friend of mine started investing in mutual funds in his IRA account around age 30. Every month he was adding to his portfolio. At 65 he had a few million dollars. The reasons for his success are: choosing the best funds, discipline in adding to the portfolio once a month irrespective of the net asset value of these funds and the snowballing effect of growth over 35 years.

Better than this story is about another friend of mine who started investing in S&P 500 index at age 35. He was adding money every month irrespective of the price of S&P 500 index.

At 65 he retired with several million dollars. He chose S&P 500 index over mutual funds is because the cost of owning index funds is much lower than the expense ratio of mutual funds and the ease of investing in index funds. Also, most mutual funds do not beat S&P 500 index.

Better than investing in S&P 500 index is investing in QQQ. In the past 15 years QQQ has beaten S&P 500 hands down. It has beaten DIA (which tracks Dow Jones Industrial Average) and IWM which tracks Russell 2000 small cap index). It has even beaten Warren Buffett's Berkshire Hathaway A shares. Please see the table below.

| SYMBOL | START DATE | START PRICE | END DATE | END PRICE | % PRICE CHANGE | % ANNUALIZED RATE OF RETURN |
|--------|-----------|-------------|----------|-----------|----------------|------------------------------|
|        | 9/27/2004 |             | 9/27/2019 |           |                |                              |
| QQQ    |           | 34.5        |          | 187.03    | 442.12         | 29.46                        |
| BRKA   |           | 86.2        |          | 311.45    | 261.31         | 17.41                        |
| VTI    |           | 53.38       |          | 150.3     | 181.57         | 12.1                         |
| IWM    |           | 55.74       |          | 151.16    | 171.21         | 11.41                        |
| DIA    |           | 100.16      |          | 267.99    | 167.56         | 11.16                        |
| SPY    |           | 110.75      |          | 295.4     | 166.73         | 11.11                        |

QQQ is Invesco QQQ Trust

SPY is SPDR S&P 500 ETF

BRKA is Berkshire Hathaway A shares (in thousands)

VTI is Vanguard Total Stock Market Index ETF

IWM is iShares Russell 2000 Index ETF

DIA is SPDR Dow Jones Industrial Average ETF

# QQQ Invesco QQQ Trust

The above is a weekly chart of QQQ courtesy of Stockcharts.com (charts, tools and education are available free and with subscription). Even though stock market has dips on and off look at the growth of the price at a 45* angle! It is very impressive.

Even if the market goes down for a few months or even a few years, the market always will come back and make new highs. Bear markets do not last forever and at some point the market turns around and goes up. When the market is going down you are sticking to the plan of buying QQQ, let us say monthly. Then you are dollar cost averaging. You end result will be much better than investing a lump sum once a year. You will be getting better prices of QQQ when the market goes down.

Listen to what the greatest investor of all time says. These quotations are like gems:

"If you invested in a very low-cost index fund -- where you don't put the money in at one time, but average in over 10 years -- you'll do better than 90% of people who start investing at the same time". (Warren Buffett)

"A good investor always plays the long game. Moving around is not smart in investing. Many investors make the mistake of constantly buying and selling stocks, rather than holding onto their investments to give them time to mature and potentially make more money over time". (Warren Buffett)

Buffett says, "If you hold on to a diverse selection of stocks for long enough, then the market should eventually trend upward. I know what markets are going to do over a long period of time: They're going to go up. But in terms of what's going to happen in a day or a week or a month or a year even, I've never felt that I knew it and I've never felt that was important,"

Let me ask you a question. Have you made 29% per year in the past 15 years by investing on your own, especially by buying and selling stocks? If not please consider following this method to victory.

Starting to invest earlier than later makes a huge difference in the final outcome. Let us go to our example of investing $6000 a year in tax deferred plan at the beginning of the year, for 35 years (from age 30 to 65) at a growth rate of 29% a year, you will have at age 65 $ 242,662,371! I used the compound interest calculator at www.moneychimp.com.

Instead if you start at age of 35 ard invest for 30 years (from age 35 to 65) at a growth rate of 29% a year, you will have at age 65, $ 67,909,573. Still you have over $67 million.

In the above method, I have usec only an investment of $6,000 per year. Of course, you can invest more for your retirement. Please consult your account, who will create the right retirement plan for you. Imagine if you can put away $30,000 a year from age 30 to 65, at the start of the year, and it grows at 29% per year, you will have $ 1,213,311,853! over one billion dollars!!. This astronomical number is real. You please check it out. Even if you started at age 35 the end result will be $ 339,547,863, over $339 million! Let your accountant verify these figures. For above calculations, I did the additions at the start of the year.

You may have a question, what if QQQ grows only at 19% a year? If you invest $30,000 a year from age 30 to 65 you will end up with a sum of $95,838,448, not bad! What if the growth rate of QQQ is only 11.65% a year, you still w ll have $14,737,468, not shabby! (The launch date of QQQ was on 4/23/1999. Until 9/27/2019 it had grown on an average annual rate of 11.65%).

What happens if you invest monthly instead of annually? The results are even better. These were calculated using Microsoft Excel. If you invest annually $6000 at the end of the year for 35 years at a growth rate of 29%, you will have $153,579,981! (over $153 million). If you invest $500 a month for 420 months (35 years), at a growth rate of 2.42% a month (29% a year), you will have $475,050,500!! (over $475 million). What happens if you invest on the $1^{st}$ and $15^{th}$ of each month?

If you invest $250 each time, at a growth rate of 1.21% (29% a year) 840 times (35 years), you will end up with $504,444,895!! (super-duper). This illustrates the fact that investing twice a month is even better. Several leading brokerage firms allow you to buy even one share of QQQ without paying any commission. Isn't it great?

Let me calculate using Microsoft Excel for compounding. If you invest $30,000 annually at the end of the year for 35 years you will have $767,899,907 at a growth rate of 29% a year. Instead if you invest $2500 a month over 420 periods (35 years), at a growth rate of 2.42% a month (29% a year), the results are amazing……..$2,375,252,500! If you invest $1250 twice a month ($30,000 a year) at a growth rate of 1.21% (29% a year), you will have a several million more dollars!! ($2,522,224,477).

As you know, at this time, many leading brokerage firms let you buy ETFs without any commission. Every penny you invest goes to work for your retirement!!

Please have faith; close your eyes; keep following the method; be firm in your commitment; you will surely succeed.

My accountant/CPA has read this book and liked it a lot. He is a professor of accounting in a university. He asked me to address his young students who loved the data. He is very knowledgeable in the stock market and has been trading stocks, options and futures successfully. He loved my simple and a great method. He is young and has started buying QQQ every two weeks. I feel flattered and happy that my CPA has applied this method for himself! It is like attestation!!

## SUMMARY

- Even when the market goes down you will be adding to your positions and getting better prices.
- Read the quotations from the great master, Warren Buffett on long term investing.
- Investing $6000 a year from age 30 to 65 at a growth rate of 29% a year will give you a retirement nest egg of $242,662,371.
  (Compound interest calculator...www.moneychimp.com).
- If you put away $30,000 a year from age 30 to 65 at a growth rate of 29% a year, you will have $1,213,311,828! (over one billion dollars. It is real. Please calculate for yourself and start believing in this method).
- Starting to invest earlier than later makes a huge difference in the final outcome.
- The best way is to invest a fixed amount of money by buying QQQ at the ask price, on the 1st and the 15th of each month in your brokerage account where you pay no commissions. You will have humongous amount of money when you retire. Always invest in the financially sound brokerage firms and make sure that your account is SIPC insured. You look at how much each account is insured for. Eventually you may need several accounts so that each one of your accounts is insured.
- Take this book seriously. Study the book. Show it to your accountant. Then on your mark, get set, go.............to victory!

# INVESTING FOR CHILDREN'S EDUCATION

Education costs are very high and they keep going up all the time. You will be extremely happy if you plan and invest for children many years before they go to college. Due to the beauty of compounding you will be amazed by the numbers achieved when your children join college, even if you invest what looks like a small amount. Later on when you withdraw money and pay for college expenses, you do not pay any taxes. This is a significant advantage. The earlier you start investing the better the results will be.

**Coverdell ESA (Education Savings Account)**: As soon as your child is born you can get a social security number and open an ESA account in a brokerage company which is financially strong. Your contributions are limited to $2000 dollars a year. You can contribute yearly until the child is 18. The growth of the investment is not taxed. Distributions are not taxed when used for educational purposes. Distributions have to be made before the age of 30. If any money is not used for educational expenses, then the balance is taxed to the beneficiary. Please read the rules and regulations in detail from the IRS site: https://www.irs.gov/taxtopics/tc310. You can invest the money for your child. Let us say you invest $2000 a year from birth to age 18 in QQQ. QQQ has gone up by 18% annually in the last 10 years as of 2/29/2020 (information from Invesco.com website). At age of 18 your child's account will have $284,174! (I used the compound interest calculator found at www.moneychimp.com. I added the $2000 in the beginning of each year). You can check this out at this website.

**529 Plan**: A 529 plan is a tax-advantaged savings plan designed to encourage savings for future education costs. There are two types of plans: Prepaid Tuition Plans and Education Savings Plans. These accounts are offered by different brokerage firms. You should carefully review the offering circular of each plan and discuss with the broker in detail. There are fees associated with these plans. Many different plans are available and hey invest in mutual funds, exchange traded funds or principal protected bank product. You can choose whatever product you like. I like to recommend investing in large cap ETF funds. In the long run they will give you the best returns. You have to compare the results of such program in different brokerage firms and choose the best one.

Many states offer tax benefits for contributions to a 529 plan. Growth in these accounts are not subject to federal income tax and in many cases state income tax. If the 529 plan withdrawals are not used for qualified higher education expenses or tuition for elementary or secondary schools, they will be subject to state and federal income taxes and an additional 10% tax penalty on the earnings. Please visit the following site and read

thoroughly the rules and regulations:
https://www.sec.gov/reportspubs/investor-publications/investorpubsintro529htm.html

# TAXATION

What is the difference between death and taxes? Congress doesn't meet every year to make death worse! (Unijokes.com). It is very important that you consult your CPA before you plan your retirement. With the method of investing you have learned from this e-book; it is obvious that you are expected to make a lot of money in the long run. So, what happens when you start withdrawing your funds? Only Roth IRAs offer tax free withdrawals. If you withdraw money from your IRA before the age of 59 ½ you will be assessed a penalty of 10% in addition to regular income tax. There are some exceptions. Based on the tax law changes, if you turned 70 ½ in 2019 you have until age 72 to start making distributions. When you withdraw funds you will be taxed according to your income tax bracket that year. There are specific rules regarding how much you should withdraw each year.

In the method you have learned from this e-book on investment the plan is to invest for the long term in QQQ. All you do is keep buying QQQ every two or four weeks at the market price at that time. So, you will get different prices based on the stock market at the time of purchase. This is basically dollar cost averaging. It is safe to do it as QQQ follows NASDAQ 100. NASDAQ 100 has 100 largest capitalized stocks in NASDAQ. So, your risk is almost non-existent. In my opinion QQQ will be around for decades and decades. When you retire your money would have grown to huge amounts, if you give time; at least more than 5 years as the market may have corrections.

What happens f your accounts are in regular non-retirement accounts? If you sell QQQ within a year you have to pay short-term capital gains tax which is the same as your ordinary income tax. But if you hold QCQ for over a year and then sell when you retire, the capital gains tax rates are 0%, 15% or 20% depending on your taxable income and filing status.

You please check with your CPA. If there is a tax advantage for you now invest in tax deferred retirement accounts. Otherwise with the plan recommended in this book, you keep on investing in a regular personal or corporate brokerage account. When you withdraw funds, you will pay much less than your regular income taxes.

# DON'TS

**If you want to achieve your goal;**

Never subscribe to financial newsletters that give you probabilities. You can flip a coin on your own.

Never listen to analysts. They are not correct most of the time. They do things to keep their jobs.

Never listen to Wall Street rumors. They are created to make you lose money.

Never get scared when the market crashes. This is when there is "Sale" in Wall Street. You will be buying QQQ at lower prices. The stock market always will come back and make new highs. Your goal is long term, at least ten years or beyond.

Never listen or discuss with anyone about your investments as this will affect your subconscious mind; thus, will affect your plans and will affect your courage to stick to your plan.

Never talk to a stock broker. Never take his/her advice. His/her company may be pushing a stock on their clients. A broker is not interested in making you rich.

Never listen to business TV channels and mute the volume if you want to watch. There is no need for you watch as you a long-term investor.

Never let anyone else manage your money. Most mutual fund managers cannot beat S&P 500. Hedge fund money managers do not make money consistently.

Never buy individual stocks as they are risky. It is hard to manage a portfolio of stocks and make good money, meaning beat S&P 500 consistently. You have to look at the long run. You cannot compete with high powered computers working which are set up by large institutions in trading. They buy and sell large volumes of stocks in a second. Individual stocks can drop significantly and wipe out your profits and principal. Warren Buffett feels that individuals have no business in owning individual stocks. He feels that individuals should own index funds. QQQ is an ETF that tracks NASDAQ-100 index.

"I will tell you how to become rich. Close the doors. Be fearful when others are greedy. Be greedy when others are fearful". (Warren Buffett)

"The wise ones bet heavily when the world offers them that opportunity. They bet big when they have the odds". (Charlie Munger)

"When the market gives you lemons, make lemonade". (Jason Zweig)

# DO'S

You be the captain of your ship. You achieved this because of your intelligence and by studying a lot. Investing is much easier if you follow a technique and do not deviate from it. You can follow this simple method to success. You need perseverance and do not use your intellect to beat the market. To meet your goal you have to use a mechanical method.

If you have any doubts about this book, let your CPA read it!

"No one will ever care as much about your money as you". (James J. Cramer)

"Learn by doing". (G. M. Loeb)

"You have got to be careful. If you don't know where you are going, because you might not get there". (Yogi Berra). So you should stick to a method.

"When you leave it to chance, then all of a sudden you don't have any more luck". (Pat Riley)

"It requires a great deal of boldness and a great deal of caution to make good fortune; and when you have got it, it requires ten times as much wit to keep it". (Nathan Mayer Rothchild)

"Discipline should always trump conviction". (James J. Cramer)

Knowledge is power. By reading books written by masters, you will become masterful, skillful and confident in your actions.

## MY RECOMMENDED BOOKS FOR YOUR READING

- "Buffettology", by Mary Buffett and David Clark.
- "The Little Book of Common Sense Investing", by John C. Bogle.

# AMAZING NEW CHANGES

I am writing this in June of 2020. In 1970s have paid even 1 2% in brokerage commission one way. Then you have to make 2.4% even to break even. Amazing changes have happened. We have to thank Charles Schwab for initiating the wave of price cuts. In October of 2019 Charles Schwab slashed their fees from $4.95 to 0. Others followed suit shortly. Imagine the tremendous advantage to us, customers. We can buy and sell even one share or thousands of shares without paying a penny and as frequently as we want.

Another great boon for investors is the possibility of buying fraction of a share. In November of 2019 Interactive Brokers became the first one to offer this feature. In January 2020 Fidelity announced the same. What is the greatness of this feature? Suppose you want to save $500 a month and you want to invest in QQQ, yes you can. A l $500 will be invested in QQQ and even if QQQ is trading at $235 you will own 2.127 shares. You can keep investing $500 a month and every penny will be invested in QQQ regardless of what it is trading at. This method is called dollar cost averaging as you know. You car invest $100 in each of stocks like Amazon, Apple, Google, etc. This is unbelievable! You can connect your brokerage account to your bank and you can transact using a cell phone! This is a superb method if you want to investment for your retirement. It is the best method to becoming a millionaire!